Kindling Spark[s]
A Religious Educ[ation for the Y]oung

By Rev. Jan Avende

©2021, Garanus Publishing
Columbus, Ohio
First Edition

**Kindling Sparks:
A Religious Education Program for Young Pagans**

By Rev. Jan Avende

©2021, Garanus Publishing
Columbus, Ohio
First Edition

Text copyright 2021 by Rev. Jan Avende
Cover image by Rev. Jan Avende
Cover design by Rev. Michael J Dangler
Rainbow sigil on back by Ian Corrigan (modified by MJD)

Find more Garanus Publishing books at

https://www.lulu.com/spotlight/garanus/

ISBN: 978-1-300-28313-3
Imprint: Lulu.com

Contents

About the Author 6
Acknowledgements 7
How To Use This Book 8
Overview of Unit Topics 10
    High Days 10
    Our Virtues 10
    Spiritual Connections 10
    Key Spirits 10
    How We Pray 11
    Parts of Ritual 11
    Consent & The Self 11
    Equality 11
    A Diverse World 11
    Environment 12
The Weekly Routine 13
    Materials 13
    Learning for the Week 13
Key Topic Description & Instruction 16
    Week 1 - Our Virtues: Hospitality 16
    Week 2 - Consent & The Self: Healthy Relationships 17
    Week 3 - Key Spirits: The Earth Mother & Loving the Earth 19
    Week 4 - How We Pray: Service 20
    Week 5 - Spiritual Connections: The Spirits Our Family Honors .. 21
    Week 6 - High Day: Autumn Equinox 23
    Week 7 - Our Virtues: Piety 24
    Week 8 - How We Pray: Devotionals & Prayer 25
    Week 9 - Parts of Ritual: The Sacred Center & The Gates 27

Week 10 - Key Spirits: Liminal Spirits 28
Week 11 - High Day: Autumn Cross Quarter 30
Week 12 - How We Pray: Ritual 31
Week 13 - Environment: Cycles & Seasons 32
Week 14 - Parts of Ritual: The Return Flow 34
Week 15 - Spiritual Connections: Important Myths 1 35
Week 16 - Parts of Ritual: Purification 37
Week 17 - Our Virtues: Courage 39
Week 18 - Equality: Understanding Fairness 40
Week 19 - High Day: Winter Solstice 41
Week 20 - Key Spirits: Ancestors 42
Week 21 - Consent & The Self: Trusted Adults 44
Week 22 - Spiritual Connections: Important Myths 2 45
Week 23 - How We Pray: Meditation & Trance 47
Week 24 - Parts of Ritual: Grounding & Centering 48
Week 25 - High Day: Winter Cross Quarter 50
Week 26 - Our Virtues: Perseverance 52
Week 27 - Equality: Racial Equity & White Privilege 53
Week 28 - Our Virtues: Fertility 55
Week 29 - Parts of Ritual: Inspiration 57
Week 30 - How We Pray: Magic 58
Week 31 - Key Spirits: Shining Ones 59
Week 32 - High Day: Spring Equinox 60
Week 33 - Our Virtues: Wisdom 62
Week 34 - Parts of Ritual: Divination & Omens 62
Week 35 - Environment: Sustainability & Conservation 64
Week 36 - Our Virtues: Integrity 65
Week 37 - High Day: Spring Cross Quarter 66
Week 38 - A Diverse World: Indigenous Religions 67

Week 39 - Equality: Cultural Appropriation 69
Week 40 - Key Spirits: Nature Spirits 70
Week 41 - Consent & The Self: Bodily Autonomy 71
Week 42 - Our Virtues: Moderation 73
Week 43 - Consent & The Self: Knowing & Caring For Me 74
Week 44 - Spiritual Connections: Ancient History 75
Week 45 - High Day: Summer Solstice 76
Week 46 - Spiritual Connections: The Wide Variety of Cultural Hearths 78
Week 47 - Key Spirits: Patrons & Allies 79
Week 48 - A Diverse World: Monotheistic Religions 80
Week 49 - A Diverse World: Polytheistic Religions 81
Week 50 - Our Virtues: Vision 82
Week 51 - A Diverse World: An Interfaith Community 83
Week 52 - High Day: Summer Cross Quarter 84

Weekly Routine Worksheet 86
Key Topics By Category (Unit Studies) 88
   High Days (8 topics) 88
   Our Virtues (9 topics) 88
   Spiritual Connections (5 topics) 89
   Key Spirits (6 topics) 89
   How We Pray (5 topics) 90
   Parts of Ritual (6 topics) 90
   Consent & The Self (4 topics) 91
   Equality (3 topics) 91
   A Diverse World (4 topics) 91
   Environment (2 topics) 92
Kindling Sparks High Day Template 93
   Notes: 93

   You will need: 93
   The Script 93
Resources & Further Reading 99
   General Resources 99
   Books on Pagan Parenting 99
   Mythology 100
   Connecting to Nature 101

About the Author

Rev. Jan Avende is a priest working with Three Cranes Grove, in Columbus, OH, and ordained through Ár nDraíocht Féin: A Druid Fellowship. They currently oversee one of the religious education programs in Ár nDraíocht Féin, focused on training magical and spiritual practitioners. In addition to having a Master's in Education, they are a talented Bard, Liturgist, and Spiritworker, with a passion for mentoring others, building resources for pagan families, and making the work that we do as pagans accessible for all. They are also a co-host of the popular podcast "Druids in Cars, Going to Festivals".

You can see more of their writing at hellenicdruid.com and support their work at patreon.com/skylark913.

Acknowledgements

Many thanks must be given to my grove's Little Oaks program, and especially Traci Auerbach, for the inspiration for this written work. I'd also like to thank my children, as they helped me pilot this program with their own experiences and learning. And finally, a special thank you to my Patreons, who supported the trial version of this work in its first year.

How To Use This Book

Welcome to the Kindling Sparks Religious Education Program! Resources for religious education for pagans are few and far between, and this program hopes to fill some of this gap for elementary-aged children. The key topics range from learning about aspects that are important to our worship, to the many ways we pray, to ways that pagans navigate the modern world. With a structured weekly routine, young pagans can work with their families towards developing a personal practice, reverence for the earth and each other, and learning about myths and spirits that are important to their family.

The Kindling Sparks Religious Education Program is laid out in a week-by-week fashion. Each week has a Key Topic that you'll focus on for the week, but there are also regular activities that form the base routine for the week. The Key Topics include a couple paragraphs that are meant to be used as direct instruction (you can read them directly to the child) to introduce the topic, as well as supplementary activities and book suggestions to help expand the child's engagement with the topic. The Activities and Reading Extensions are just suggestions, so don't feel pressured to complete every suggested activity or read every book. Additionally, for High Days there is not only a description of the High Day, but also a ritual script that can be used to celebrate the High Day.

The program is cyclical and can be started at any point in the year. As written, it begins shortly after the Summer Cross-Quarter High Day, to loosely align with the start of the traditional school year. To adapt to a different starting point families will simply need to move the weeks focusing on the High Days to the appropriate time, and work everything else in order. Additionally, the program is flexible enough that if your family has a practice that is not included in this book there is plenty of space to either add your traditions into the weekly routine or substitute a week with something of your own. The way the program is set up you are able to work through the book multiple times, following the Wheel of the Year as your child grows older. The things you do every week can shift to follow the child's interests, and the key topics are broad enough that you can deepen your child's understanding of them in subsequent years.

The program assumes your family has a hearth culture, or collection of spirits you honor. You may draw from one or many cultural influences to fill out this topic. It is meant to match what your family does and who you honor at your own altar. If your family is learning together, then the program provides a structure to begin learning about different deities, different cultures, and ways to honor them.

Overview of Unit Topics

Rather than following the week-by-week order of Key Topics, some families may want to group these topics together by larger category. An outline of this Unit Studies approach can be found in the back of the book.

High Days

This unit focuses on the eight neo-pagan high days. There are eight high days each year. These are the major holidays that we celebrate as modern pagans. They correspond to the different important points in the cycle of seasons, and are about six and a half weeks apart from each other.

Our Virtues

This unit focuses on nine different virtues. Virtues are values that we believe in that help us to lead a good life. They can help guide us when things get hard, help us make good choices, and help us develop a fulfilling spiritual life.

Spiritual Connections

There are many ways we make connections, and maintain those connections, with the spirits. In this unit we look at not only the spirits that your family honors, but also myths and stories, as well as what spirits ancient cultures honored and how those ancient cultures prayed.

Key Spirits

There are many categories of spirits, including ancestors, spirits of nature, and deities. This unit is broken down into those different, broad categories so that we can look at each in depth.

How We Pray

There are many ways that pagans pray or show devotion to the earth and the spirits. In this unit we look at not only the words that you may typically think of as prayer, but also other ways to show devotion.

Parts of Ritual

In this unit we look at the specific elements that commonly make up a full ritual. These individual pieces are divided out so that we can learn about them more in-depth.

Consent & The Self

Paganism is a religion that is heavily focused on this world, and how we interact with other people and spirits here. It is important that we understand and know ourselves in order to have safe and meaningful interactions. This unit focuses on learning about your identity and your boundaries.

Equality

In this unit we focus on ways to make our religion more inclusive, and to take responsibility for how our actions will affect others. Paganism is a civic religion, meaning it is tied to how we interact with society at large.

A Diverse World

Paganism is not the only religion in the world. This unit focuses on some of the different religions that you may encounter, as well as how these religions can all interact respectfully and peacefully.

Environment

One of the big themes in paganism is a reverence for the earth. In this unit we talk about the different scientific reasons that we celebrate the cycles of the earth, as well as ways that we can keep the earth healthy and beautiful.

The Weekly Routine

The Kindling Sparks Religious Education Program is laid out in a week-by-week fashion. Each of these has a Key Topic that you'll focus on for the week, but there are also regular activities that you'll want to make time for each week as well. In the back of this book there is an optional worksheet you can either print or copy for use each week. You can find the printable version of this page at:
https://tinyurl.com/WeeklyRoutine

Materials

You'll need minimal materials for the Key Topic activities, most of which can be found around your house or outside. There are some additional things I recommend acquiring to enrich your experience:

- A journal or sketchbook: Your child will use this for multiple activities throughout the year. There is no need to get a different one for each category unless you want to. I recommend either an unlined sketchbook, or a primary composition book (picture space on the top, lines on the bottom) for younger children. This will allow you room to both write and draw.
- A Nature ID Guide: one of the things you'll be doing each week is observing nature. I recommend getting a local field guide to wildlife in your area. You can get separate ones for plants, birds, animals, etc., or you can find one that comes in a set. The Resources section in the back of this book has some recommendations.

Learning for the Week

Key Topic

This is the special topic that changes each week. Details about the Key Topic are in the following section under their own headings. You may need to flip some of the weeks around to make sure that your High Day Key Topics occur during the actual High Day, as this will shift from year to year. There may or may not be anything specific to record in your journal for the Key Topic each week. Follow your child's lead if they'd like to write or draw about something from the week.

Nature Observation

Make time at least once each week to get outside and do some nature observation. You can either watch the weather and plan for a nice day to spend outside, or encourage enjoying nature in all of its presentations by dressing for the weather and heading outside in varying conditions. You will also keep a Nature Journal to write or draw about what you see on your nature walks. Some things you might observe are animals, plants, insects, different parts of the ecosystem, weather, etc. Bring your field guide with you to try and identify unfamiliar plants or animals. Try sketching the distinguishing features of these plants or animals in your Nature Journal.

Deity Focus

Each week you will choose a different deity to focus on and learn about. You can research what cultures followed them, read some of their myths, look at pictures and statues of them, etc. You may end up wanting to make art about that deity, or build a shrine to them. Follow your child's lead about what they might be interested in, and look for deities that align with that interest. You should also make sure to include deities that are important to your family.

Weekly Reflection

One of the goals of Kindling Sparks is to not only teach our children about our religion, but to also help them learn to interact with the world as a pagan. To that end, encourage them to write or draw a weekly reflection in their journal. Some good questions to answer are "How have I embodied hospitality this week?" and "How have I been a good steward of the earth this week?" Feel free to add your own questions, or encourage your child to respond in their own way on how they've incorporated paganism into their life this week.

Key Topic Description & Instruction

Week 1 - Our Virtues: Hospitality

Weekly Routine:

- ☐ Key Topic
- ☐ Nature Observation
- ☐ Deity Focus
- ☐ Weekly Reflection

Key Topic Direct Instruction:

What are virtues?

Virtues are important values and beliefs that help us act as good people in the world.

What is Hospitality?

Hospitality is a way of saying that we should be kind to each other. It's much like the golden rule: "Treat others the way you'd like to be treated". When one person does something nice, sometimes the other person will do something nice for them in return. But, the important thing to remember is that we do nice things for others without expecting them to do something for us. It's important to be a kind person even when no one is watching. We have these kinds of relationships with our family, friends, and neighbors, but we can also have them with the Gods and Spirits.

Activities:

- Do something nice for someone else. You can share a favorite toy, write a letter to a neighbor, friend, or family member, or help out with a chore you don't normally do.

- Play a game where you take turns. Board games are a great choice. If you have several kids together an outdoor game like tag, hide & seek, or red light-green light would be a good choice.
- Have your stuffed animals or dolls play a game where they take turns doing nice things for each other
- Do a ritual and make offerings (like special pictures you drew, oil, or grain), and receive blessings (like water) in return.

Reading Extensions:

- "Do Unto Otters" by Laurie Keller
- "Hakeem is a Good Neighbor" by Cathy Vargo
- "Be Kind" by Pat Miller
- "What does it mean to be kind?" by Rana DiOrio
- "Be kind: 125 kind things to say & do: you can make the world a happier place!" by Naomi Shulman

Week 2 - Consent & The Self: Healthy Relationships

Weekly Routine:

☐ Key Topic
☐ Nature Observation
☐ Deity Focus
☐ Weekly Reflection

Key Topic Direct Instruction:

What does a Healthy Relationship look like?

When we have healthy relationships, we're being hospitable to others, and they are being hospitable to us. Do you remember what hospitality means from last week? In a healthy relationship our friends won't ask us to do things that make us uncomfortable. Adults won't make us do things that make us worried or scared, and they won't ask us to keep secrets that make us uncomfortable. In healthy relationships we're allowed to speak up about the things that make us feel safe and unsafe. We can tell we're in a healthy relationship when it feels good to be around the other person, and it doesn't make us uncomfortable, scared, or worried. We have respect for each other, don't make fun of each other, and don't tell lies.

Discretion, Surprises, and Secrets

Discretion means there are things parents get to talk to their kids about, like religion, but this also includes things like Santa, the Tooth Fairy, etc. (adults: if your kids still believe in these, you might leave those out of the discussion this year). We don't normally talk about these things outside of our family and trusted adults. A trusted adult is someone that both you and your parents or guardians know and someone that will never ask you to keep a secret.

Surprises are exciting things we keep hidden for a short time and they make others happy. With a surprise, everyone finds out about it. Some surprises are things like presents, and birthday parties. Surprises should never make you uncomfortable, scared, or worried.

Secrets are things that some people keep hidden that probably shouldn't be hidden. If someone has a secret there is a reason that probably isn't good or safe. If someone asks you to keep a secret you should find help from a trusted adult. You can also tell others that you don't keep secrets if they ask.

Activities:

- Have your adult ask you to do silly and outrageous things, and practice telling them no.
- Play a game where you make faces with different emotions and take turns guessing what the other is feeling
- Draw a picture of or write a story about two friends being kind to each other
- Make a friendship chain or friendship handprint wreath out of construction paper, where each link or

wreath piece says some quality that you like in a friend (ex: shares, kind, smiles a lot, gives good hugs, etc.)

Reading Extensions:
- Elephant & Piggie books by Mo Willems
- "Deena is a Good Friend" by Sofia Rory
- "Some Secrets Should Never Be Kept" by Jayneen Sanders

Week 3 - Key Spirits: The Earth Mother & Loving the Earth

Weekly Routine:

- ☐ Key Topic
- ☐ Nature Observation
- ☐ Deity Focus
- ☐ Weekly Reflection

Key Topic Direct Instruction:

Who is the Earth Mother?

One of the primary deities that we honor is the Earth Mother. She provides for us, nurtures us, and gives us a home. While we arguably cannot be surrounded by the other aspects of our religion at all times, the Earth Mother is ever present. She existed before we arrived here, and will exist beyond our parting. In our formal rites we honor her both first and last, and she is given any additional offerings we don't use after the rite.

How do we honor the Earth?

We honor the Earth by being kind to her. It is kind of like the hospitality we've talked about before, but there are specific things we can do to honor the earth. We can make sure we never litter, and pick up litter whenever we see it. We can conserve our resources by turning off things like the lights and the water when we're not using them. We can make sure that we don't buy things we don't need, that we reuse whatever we can, and that when we have to get rid of something we make sure to recycle or compost it if we're able. We can also do things with the earth to honor her, like planting or weeding in our gardens.

Activities:
- Draw a picture of or write a story about the Earth Mother
- Plant, weed, or harvest in your garden
- Go on a clean-up hike

Reading Extension:
- "The Lorax" by Dr. Seuss
- "Thank You Earth" by April Pulley Sayre
- "I Can Save the Earth" by Alison Inches
- "Earth Mother" by Ellen Jackson
- "The Mess That We Made" by Michelle Lord
- "Compost Stew: An A to Z Recipe for the Earth" by Mary McKenna Siddals
- "You Are Never Alone" by Elin Kelsey

Week 4 - How We Pray: Service

Weekly Routine:

☐ Key Topic
☐ Nature Observation
☐ Deity Focus
☐ Weekly Reflection

Key Topic Direct Instruction:

There are lots of ways to pray, and you might be most familiar with saying words and making offerings, but there are other things we can do too. One way to pray is to do something that a specific spirit or deity would like. Like when we plant trees or flowers, that is one way of praying to the Earth Mother. When we volunteer to help families who don't have as much as we do, that is one way to honor a deity who takes care of people. When we volunteer at an animal shelter, that is one way to honor the nature spirits. There are lots of things we can do to pray through service.

Activities:

- Plant some trees, bushes, or other plants
- Join a group to pull out invasive plants, or weed in your garden
- Volunteer at an animal shelter (there are many that have parent-child dog walking teams)
- Go on a nature hike and pick up litter
- Pick a different service project (see reading extension)

Reading Extensions:

- "Can We Help?" by George Ancona
- "The Kid's Guide to Service Projects" by Barbara Lewis

Week 5 - Spiritual Connections: The Spirits Our Family Honors

Weekly Routine:

☐ Key Topic
☐ Nature Observation
☐ Deity Focus
☐ Weekly Reflection

Key Topic Direct instruction:

Every pagan family has special spirits they pray to and honor. Sometimes they all come from the same ancient culture, and sometimes they don't. These special spirits can be deities, ancestors, nature spirits, or somewhere in between.

Our Spirits:

Talk about the special spirits in your family, and if you have a family altar talk about who is represented on that altar.

Activities:

- Build your own altar (we'll add to it in later weeks as we learn more)
- Draw a picture of or write a story about a special deity or spirit
- Make a toilet paper roll icon for your deity to put on your altar. You can create one of your own, or use a template from Werkelwald
    - Toilet Paper Roll Deity Images (by Birgit Reinhartz): http://werkelwald.de/etwas-respektlos-aber-dennoch-klorollengoetter/ (website is in German, but downloads for the pictures are easy to find)
- Find something in nature that your special deity or spirit would like
- Create and make an offering to your special deity or spirit

Reading Extensions:

- "What is an Altar?" by Rowen Moss
- A myth or story about a deity your family honors would be especially appropriate this week.
    - "Myths, Legends, & Sacred Stories" by Philip Wilkinson - short summaries/retellings for a large number of famous myths across the world. Contains both historical pictures, as well as artistic interpretations.

- D'Aulaires' Books of Myths (there's one for Greek and one for Norse) - brief retellings of famous myths

Week 6 - High Day: Autumn Equinox

Weekly Routine:

- ☐ Key Topic
- ☐ Nature Observation
- ☐ Deity Focus
- ☐ Weekly Reflection

Key Topic Direct Instruction:

Autumn Equinox is the second of the three harvest festivals. It begins the dark half of the year, as it is the day when the day and night are the same length, but the nights will become longer from this day on. During this time of the Autumn Equinox, we pause to give thanks to the bountiful harvests of the world around us. It is a time for reflection on the joys of the summer months and the light half of the year, and a time for contemplation of the coming hardships of the dark half of the year.

Activities:

- Perform a ritual for Autumn Equinox
  - https://charteroakadf.org/family-resources/
  - Kindling Sparks Ritual Template (found in the back of the book)
- Go apple picking
- Look for trees that have changing color leaves. If any are on the ground, press in wax paper
- Decorate your altar for the season
- Read myths about harvest deities

Reading Extensions:
- "Autumn Equinox: The Enchantment of Mabon" by Ellen Dugan
- "The Autumn Equinox: Celebrating the Harvest" by Ellen Jackson
- "We Gather Together" by Wendy Pfeffer
- "Goodbye Summer, Hello Autumn" by Kenard Pak

Week 7 - Our Virtues: Piety

Weekly Routine:

- ☐ Key Topic
- ☐ Nature Observation
- ☐ Deity Focus
- ☐ Weekly Reflection

Key Topic Direct Instruction:

Piety is one of our virtues, which are the things that help make us good people. Piety is what we are doing when we pray and honor the deities and spirits. Remember there are lots of ways to pray. We've talked about praying through service and will talk about devotionals and spoken & written prayers next week. Because service can be the things we do to honor the deities and spirits, piety can also be things that we do for them. We can also be pious when we keep our virtues, like hospitality.

Activities:

- Draw a picture of or write a story about what it looks like to be pious
- Share a story about someone who you think demonstrates piety
- Pray to a special deity from your family's collection of spirits

- When you're reading one of the extension books, talk with your caring adult about what piety looks like in different cultures and religions

Reading Extensions:
- "The Kid's Book of World Religions" by Jennifer Glossop - a good overview of many world religions. Very little Christian bias. Neo-paganism is not included.
- "The Usborne Book of World Religions" by Susan Meredith

Week 8 - How We Pray: Devotionals & Prayer

Weekly Routine:

☐ Key Topic
☐ Nature Observation
☐ Deity Focus
☐ Weekly Reflection

Key Topic Direct Instruction:

What is a devotional?

Devotionals are the set of actions and words we use in order to honor the spirits. The most common kind of devotional is lighting a candle and saying or thinking a short prayer. During a devotional you can also make offerings to the spirit or spirits you're honoring. One thing that makes a devotional different from a ritual or a prayer is that we're not asking for anything. We're just expressing our love and devotion to the spirit.

What is prayer?

Prayer is what we do to honor the spirits, and also how we ask them for help in our lives. The most common way to pray is by using our words. A simple prayer can be written or spoken by describing the spirits we're honoring, asking for help with something or expressing our appreciation, and then thanking the spirit.

Many Ways to Pray

A lot of people sit or stand a certain way when they pray, and a lot of times they change where they put their hands and arms. Some people like to play music or sing about their special spirits in order to pray to them. Other people like to dance so that they can feel their special spirits with them.

Activities:

- Write or speak a prayer to your special spirit, or one of your family's special spirits
- Have an adult help you light a candle to pray
- Create or find something that would make a good offering to your special spirit, or one of your family's special spirits
- Learn about and practice different body positions people might use when they pray (ex: orans position, palms facing up or down, palms together, kneeling, arms raised, bowing, etc.)
- Listen and dance to some pagan music
  - Damh the Bard, SJ Tucker, Kellianna, Hugin the Bard, and Raffi's "Evergreen, Everblue" album are some popular options
- Play some music for your special spirit. Drums, shakers, and other percussion instruments are good choices

Reading Extensions:

- "Before Morning" by Joyce Sidman - see the back page of the book for a discussion about invocations

- "How to Write an Invocation" by Rev. Jan Avende: https://hellenicdruid.com/2015/08/25/how-to-write-an-invocation/

Week 9 - Parts of Ritual: The Sacred Center & The Gates

Weekly Routine:

- ☐ Key Topic
- ☐ Nature Observation
- ☐ Deity Focus
- ☐ Weekly Reflection

Key Topic Direct Instruction:

The Sacred Center

The Sacred Center is the place at the middle of the Cosmos that we go to when we pray and talk to the spirits. Making the Sacred Center is the part of ritual when we line up all the realms so we can stand at the Center of the Cosmos. Most often the Fire is in the middle of our Sacred Center, and we can see the circle of the Sacred Center by looking at how far the light from our Fire stretches.

A lot of times the Sacred Center is made up of a Fire, Well, and/or Tree. The Fire connects us to the Shining Ones (the Deities). You can use a candle (flame or battery-powered) to represent the Fire. The Well, which is full of water, connects us to the Ancestors. You can use a small dish of water to represent the Well. The Tree, or some other type of sacred pillar or stone, connects us to the Nature Spirits and all the realms. The Tree is like a great line of communication that connects us to the Ancestors below, the Nature Spirits here, and the Shining Ones above. You can use a stick, stone, picture, or sculpture to represent the Tree.

The Gates

The Gates are the supernatural or imaginary doors that separate our world from the otherworld, or the world of the spirits. When we open the Gates we connect our Fire, Well, and Tree to the places where the Three Kindreds live. We work with a Gatekeeper (a liminal, or "in-between" spirit) to help us make those connections. We'll learn more about them next week.

Activities:

- Create or find representations of the Fire, Well, and/or Tree to put on your altar
- Put a candle or lantern on a piece of paper, turn out the lights, and draw a circle around it to mark where the shadows start. Talk about how it's a fuzzy boundary (there are degrees of darkness). Turn the lights back on and draw the rest of your ritual space inside the circle.

Week 10 - Key Spirits: Liminal Spirits

Weekly Routine:

- ☐ Key Topic
- ☐ Nature Observation
- ☐ Deity Focus
- ☐ Weekly Reflection

Key Topic Direct Instruction:

What is a Liminal Spirit?

Liminal means "in-between." A liminal spirit is one who is really good at helping us communicate with other spirits. These spirits are sometimes called Gatekeepers, Intermediaries, Intersessional Spirits, Spirit Guides, of Psychopomps. We work with them in our ritual structure because they help us focus our rituals and call to the spirits we're trying to contact. It's kind of like they are in charge of the telephone to the other spirits. Sometimes we can use the telephone on our own, but it's easier if someone helps us remember what number to call. And, spirits that we talk to all the time, we memorize their number, and don't need as much help talking to them.

Who is a Gatekeeper?

A Gatekeeper is a spirit that stands at the crossroads and aids us in opening, or holding open, the gates between worlds. Any being that can walk between the worlds or exist in all the worlds is able to work with us as a Gatekeeper.

Who is a Gatekeeper in our Family's tradition?

- Talk about who your family works with most often as a Gatekeeper. Some examples:
  - Garanus Crane
  - Manannán mac Lir
  - Hekate
  - Hermes
  - Janus
  - Heimdall

Activities:

- Draw a picture of or write a story about the Gatekeeper doing their job
- Play a game where one person pretends to be the Gatekeeper. Everyone else chants "Open the Gates, Open the Gate". Then the "Gatekeeper shouts "Let the Gates be Open" and everyone runs past the Gatekeeper. First one there is the next Gatekeeper (much like Red Light, Green Light).
- Get out some play scarves and pretend like you can see the gates opening, and talk to the spirits after you've moved the scarves out of the way.
- Read a story about a Gatekeeper spirit (check out the mythology books in the Resources section at the back of this book)

Week 11 - High Day: Autumn Cross Quarter

Weekly Routine:

- ☐ Key Topic
- ☐ Nature Observation
- ☐ Deity Focus
- ☐ Weekly Reflection

Key Topic Direct Instruction:

The Ancestors

The autumn cross quarter, often called Samhain, is a time of remembrance for the dead. It is referred to as the time when the veil between the worlds is thinnest, and thus it is a liminal (remember that word? It means "in-between") time when we can more easily communicate with our Ancestors: the Mighty Dead, the Ancient Wise, and the Beloved Dead. The Mighty Dead are people like heroes from mythical stories, and we ask for their help to be brave when we do hard things in our life. The Ancient Wise are people who were very smart or wise when they lived, and we ask for their knowledge to help us lead better lives. The Beloved Dead are our friends and family that we know who have died, and we ask them to keep loving and supporting us just like they did when they were alive.

The Third Harvest Festival

Samhain is also the final of the three harvest festivals when the animals that won't make it through the winter are culled, or removed, from the herd. With that final bounty of food, it is often a time for a great feast honoring those who have passed. During that feast people will often share stories about the Ancestors that are important to them.

Activities:
- Perform a ritual for Autumn Equinox
  - https://charteroakadf.org/family-resources/
  - Kindling Sparks Ritual Template (found in the back of the book)
- Carve a pumpkin
- Decorate masks to trick the spirits into leaving you alone
- Decorate your altar for the season
- Read myths about fairies, particularly about the two courts of fairies that move during season changes.

Reading Extensions:
- "Child of Faerie, Child of Earth" by Jane Yolen
- "Halloween Is…" by Gail Gibbons
- "Halloween" by Dana Meachen Rau
- "The Memory Tree" by Britta Teckentrup

Week 12 - How We Pray: Ritual

Weekly Routine:

- ☐ Key Topic
- ☐ Nature Observation
- ☐ Deity Focus
- ☐ Weekly Reflection

Key Topic Direct Instruction:

A ritual, or a rite, is a more formal and fancy way to pray. It has a set structure and order to the way we do things, has many parts, and each part does a specific thing to help make the prayer stronger. These scripts or specified parts help make our rituals predictable and easy to remember because they specify each thing that we do in ritual and when we do it.

We've already learned about the Sacred Center. Ritual nearly always happens in a sacred space, and there are many ways to make a space sacred. Most often in our rites we light a fire and open the gates to make a space sacred. Sometimes we light incense or sprinkle water around.

In upcoming weeks we'll learn more about some of the different parts of ritual.

Ritual vs. Routine

A ritual is similar to a routine because both of them are things we do that have a specific order to tasks. The difference is that a ritual is done to make us feel connected to the spirits, and a routine is just something we do regularly in a specific way. One of the neat things you can do is take a routine (like all the steps you take getting ready for bed), and add a ritual element to it (like speaking a prayer before laying down).

Activities:

- Perform a ritual to ask for blessings. (you can use the high day script and modify it to be less seasonally specific)
- Add a ritual element to a routine you already have.
- Practice writing or drawing out all the specific steps to take to do a regular task (like the instructions for making a peanut butter sandwich). Then talk about how remembering those steps in order is like how we perform ritual steps in order.

Week 13 - Environment: Cycles & Seasons

Weekly Routine:

☐ Key Topic

- ☐ Nature Observation
- ☐ Deity Focus
- ☐ Weekly Reflection

Key Topic Direct Instruction:

What is the Lunar Cycle?

The Lunar Cycle is the way the moon changes phases throughout the month. At one end the moon is dark and you can't see it, then it slowly becomes full and looks like a giant glowing ball, and then at the other end of the cycle it gets dark again. Then the cycle starts over again, continuously going from dark to full to dark to full, over and over again. One of the things we celebrate as pagans are the different phases of the moon.

What is the Solar Cycle? What are the Seasons?

The Solar Cycle is the way the High Days are laid out throughout the year to follow the seasons. Because the Earth is tilted while it revolves around the Sun, and the sunlight hits the Earth differently based on how the Earth is tilted, we experience different seasons. They are Autumn, Winter, Spring, and Summer. One of the things we celebrate as pagans are the changing of the seasons.

Activities:

- Use ping pong balls, chocolate sandwich cookies, paper plates, or similar to decorate and show each phase of the moon
- Make a 'phases of the moon' flipbook
- Draw and label a tree to look like each season. This is a great opportunity for a multimedia craft (use puff balls, tissue paper, fingerpaints/handprints, etc.)
- Read, draw, act out, or retell a myth about why seasons change

Reading Extensions:

- "The Phases of the Moon" by George Pendergast

- "Ring of Earth" by Jane Yolen
- "A Year of Seasons" by George Pendergast
- "Earth Cycles" by Michael Ross
- "Tap the Magic Tree" by Christie Matheson
- "Demeter and Persephone" by Hugh Lupton
- "Tree" by Britta Teckentrup
- "Sunshine Makes the Seasons" by Franklyn M. Branley

Week 14 - Parts of Ritual: The Return Flow

Weekly Routine:

☐ Key Topic
☐ Nature Observation
☐ Deity Focus
☐ Weekly Reflection

Key Topic Direct Instruction:

The Return Flow:

The Return Flow, sometimes called Receiving the Blessing, is one of the steps in our ritual structure. This is the part of ritual after we have made offerings to the spirits. In the same way that we gave offerings to them, this is their way of giving offerings to us. It completes the circle of the hospitality relationship. We were kind and hospitable to them, so now they are being kind and hospitable to us. In the Return Flow we ask for the blessings of the spirits, we hallow (use magic to make sacred) the blessings so they are in a form we can use. Most often we do this with a food or drink. Then we take the blessings, often by eating or drinking the thing we have hallowed.

Energy Raising:

One way that we hallow our food or drink to fill it with the blessings of the Kindreds is by raising energy to make the magic easier and more powerful. Energy is the force that makes things happen, and there are many ways to imagine it so you can sense it. You may imagine a colored light surrounding an object or person, or you may hear a sound getting louder as the energy gets bigger. One of the ways we raise energy to use in our magic is by making noise. A lot of people like to hum louder and louder. Other people will clap or rub their hands together until they feel warm. You can also use instruments, like a drum, to make music that will raise energy.

Activities:

- Make a special food or drink that you could use in the Return Flow (this is a great opportunity to involve your kids in the kitchen)
- Have a simple ritual where you make offerings and receive blessings in return using a special food or drink
- Write or draw the blessings/gifts the Kindreds gave you on clean stone, rock, shell, or similar in permanent marker. Then drop this stone in a cup of water and drink the water you've just blessed.
- Pick your favorite way to raise energy, and then practice wrapping your hands around a cup of water to transfer that energy to the cup. See if you can imagine it flowing from your hands into the water.

Week 15 - Spiritual Connections: Important Myths 1

Weekly Routine:

☐ Key Topic
☐ Nature Observation
☐ Deity Focus
☐ Weekly Reflection

Key Topic Direct Instruction:

What are myths?

Myths are stories that we tell to help explain the way the world works, or to tell about important people in our history and spirituality. A lot of myths involve gods and goddesses, or other magical spirits.

Important types of myths

There are a lot of categories of myths that you can read or hear about. Your family may not have a specific myth for each important thing, but that's okay. If you're interested you can start exploring the myths of your family's important spirits, and you can explore the myths outside your family's important spirits. Some types of myths tell about the creation of the world, or how humans came to be. Some types of myths talk about the importance of hospitality and being nice to strangers. Some types of myths explain how we learned certain things (like how to make fire), or how we receive the blessings of the Gods. Some types of myths talk about fighting that happened between different groups of spirits or gods. Some types of myths tell the story of a hero and their adventures. Some types of myths talk about what happens after we die.

Activities:

- Read a myth that is important to your family. These will depend on what is available in your primary pantheon and what is important to your family. Possible options include:
    - Creation myths (humans, or the world in general)
    - Winning the waters/gaining wisdom myths
    - Myths that show importance of hospitality
    - Myths about a divine war
    - Myths about deities/spirits important to your family
    - Stories relating to the hero's cycle/monomyth
    - Stories about the afterlife

- Draw a picture telling your favorite part of a myth you read or heard
- Retell or act out part of one of the myths you read or heard
- Talk about any lessons you might have learned from the myth you read or heard. Is there a certain way you should act or behave based on what that myth says?

Reading Extensions:

- "Treasury of Greek Mythology" by Donna Jo Napoli
- "Treasury of Norse Mythology" by Donna Jo Napoli
- "Celtic Mythology" by Philip Freeman
- "Myths, Legends, & Sacred Stories" by Philip Wilkinson
- "Celtic Mythology: History for Kids" by Dinobibi Publishing

Week 16 - Parts of Ritual: Purification

Weekly Routine:

☐ Key Topic
☐ Nature Observation
☐ Deity Focus
☐ Weekly Reflection

Key Topic Direct Instruction:

What is purification?

Purification is a fancy way of saying "clean," and in ritual it is what we do before we start. We want to have a clean body and a clear mind before we begin a big ritual.

How do I purify myself?

There are many ways to have a clean body. You probably can already guess that washing your hands is a good way to start, but a special way to have a clean body for ritual is by using smoke. An adult can help you light some incense and move your body through the smoke. While smoke cleansing like this is good for ritual cleanliness, it can't replace your regular bath.

To have a clean mind we want to get all the extra thoughts and worries out of our brain so we can focus on doing a ritual and praying. A lot of times this also means getting all the extra energy out of our bodies. We can let go of our worries by putting them away for a little while. Often this is easier to do if we tone, or hum, while we're doing this. It gives our brain something else to focus on. We can let the extra energy out of our bodies by shaking our arms and legs or stretching.

Activities:

- Wash your hands while singing your favorite hand washing song.
- Have your caring adult help you light some incense and dance in the smoke.
- Write or draw your extra thoughts and worries on tissue paper, then blow them away into a trash can using a straw
- Write or draw your extra thoughts and worries on paper, and then pack them one by one into a bag
- Listen to Raffi's "Shake Your Sillies Out" and dance away all your extra energy

Reading Extensions:

- "Wash Your Hands!" by Tony Ross

Week 17 - Our Virtues: Courage

Weekly Routine:

☐ Key Topic
☐ Nature Observation
☐ Deity Focus
☐ Weekly Reflection

Key Topic Direct Instruction:

Courage is when we are able to do something even though it is hard or scary. Courage is when we are brave and willing to try something new, or stand up for what we believe in. It's important to remember that courage doesn't mean you're not scared of something, but rather it means you're still willing to try even though you're scared. It can also mean that even if you fail at something that you're willing to try again.

Courage isn't only doing physical things that are scary, but it can also mean to stand up and speak out when we need to. It can take courage to speak up when we see something wrong, but that doesn't mean we should try to make things right.

Activities:

- With your caring adult, think of something that is scary or hard, and brainstorm ways you can try to do or experience that thing. Then with their help, do it!
- Role play/pretend play with a friend or your caring adult something that could be scary or hard to do, and imagine what it looks and feels like to succeed
- Pretend you are a superhero, and decide what special powers you have that let you be brave
- Read a story about a person or animal that is brave

Reading Extensions:

- "Courage" by Julie Murray

- "Courage" by Kimberley Jane Pryor
- "The Juice Box Bully" by Robert Sornson
- "Be Bold!" by Elsie Olson

Week 18 - Equality: Understanding Fairness

Weekly Routine:

☐ Key Topic
☐ Nature Observation
☐ Deity Focus
☐ Weekly Reflection

Key Topic Direct Instruction:

Equity is a word that is often confused with equality. Equality means everyone should be treated the same regardless of differences, equity means giving everyone what they need to succeed. One simple example to help understand the difference is what you do when someone gets hurt. If you fall and scrape your knee, then you need a band aid. If your friend falls and breaks their arm, while it would be equal to give them a band aid, what they actually need is a cast. Giving them a cast is equity because they need something different than you to help them heal.

It's important to understand that fairness is when everybody is given what they need, in order to do what they're trying to do. Just because two people receive different things doesn't mean it's unfair, if they're trying to achieve the same goal.

Activities:

- Brainstorm with your caring adult some hard tasks that might require different things to help someone do. [Some examples: putting on shoes (velcro vs tying), reading a book (audio vs text), or riding a bike (how many wheels?)]

- Do something helpful for someone in need

Reading Extensions:
- "Activists Assemble - We Are All Equal" by Shannon Weber
- "Civil Rights: Then and Now - A Timeline of the Fight for Equality in America" by Kristina Brooke Daniele

Week 19 - High Day: Winter Solstice

Weekly Routine:

☐ Key Topic
☐ Nature Observation
☐ Deity Focus
☐ Weekly Reflection

Key Topic Direct Instruction:

Winter Solstice, often called Yule, is the longest night of the year. It is often seen as a time of death and rebirth. It is the darkest and longest night (remember this from when we talked about seasons?), but from that point on the days will get longer each day, and so hope is renewed. At this point we know that the winter will not keep getting darker and that it will end. One of the main themes with Winter Solstice is "hope" because things will start getting brighter again.

Sometimes the winter can start to feel lonely, since it gets harder to go play outside with our friends. We often end up spending more time with our families around this time. It is a great time to play games and tell stories that help us feel more connected to the people we live with.

Activities:
- Have a fancy dinner by candle light

- Have your adult hide candles around your house and then go on a hunt to find them. Light them in a safe spot after you've found all of them to "find the light"
- Listen to or read a story about hope with your family
- Leave an electric candle on overnight during the night of the Winter Solstice to keep the light going through the darkest night
- Perform a ritual for the Winter Solstice
    - https://charteroakadf.org/family-resources/
    - Kindling Sparks Ritual Template (found in the back of the book)
- Use craft supplies to create a sun
- Listen to or read a story or myth about the Winter Solstice

Reading Extensions:

- "The Shortest Day: Celebrating the Winter Solstice" by Wendy Pfeffer
- "The Winter Solstice" by Ellen Jackson
- "Singing Away the Dark" by Caroline Woodward
- "The Longest Night" Marion Dane Bauer
- "Lucia and the Light" by Phyllis Root
- "Sing the Cold Winter Away" by Kathy Reid-Naiman (music selection)

Week 20 - Key Spirits: Ancestors

Weekly Routine:

☐ Key Topic
☐ Nature Observation
☐ Deity Focus
☐ Weekly Reflection

Key Topic Direct Instruction:

Who are the Ancestors?

The Ancestors are those people who went before us in the world and influenced our lives in a positive way. They can be people like friends and family members who have died. We remember them and honor them and they bless us with their wisdom and love.

The three broad categories we talk about are the Ancient Wise, the Mighty Dead, and the Beloved Dead. The Ancient Wise are those ancestors who had special wisdom or intelligence in their life, and as such they now have knowledge and skills beyond what we know that can help us in our life.

The Mighty Dead are the heroes. They are not only those heroes we learn about in myth, but also the people who have helped to shape our world, culture, and society. The heroes of mythology have aided the growth and development of culture by being strong or and brave, or by gaining wisdom to share with us. The heroes of modern times have helped us through scientific discoveries, exploration, or work in social justice (as some examples). The Mighty Dead are those who've experienced the world, strove to make it a better place, and because of that have had their stories told to many people.

The Beloved Dead are those who have some direct connection to us. They may be those ancestors that we are related to by blood, such as our parents, grandparents, and great-grandparents. They may also be close friends who we care for. The Beloved Dead are those who influenced our lives in a positive way.

Activities:

- Look at old family photo albums & tell stories
- Build an ancestor box
- Research cultural heroes/famous people
- Learn a craft, song, game, or food that your ancestors would have known

Reading Extension:
- "The Kindreds" by Rev. Kathleen Pezza
  - https://www.lulu.com/en/us/shop/rev-kathleen-pezza/the-kindred/paperback/product-17ge67e8.html
- "The Dandelion's Tale" by Kevin Sheehan
- "Chester Raccoon and the Acorn Full of Memories" by Audrey Penn
- "The Memory Tree" by Britta Teckentrup
- "A Last Goodbye" by Elin Kelsey

Week 21 - Consent & The Self: Trusted Adults

Weekly Routine:

☐ Key Topic
☐ Nature Observation
☐ Deity Focus
☐ Weekly Reflection

Key Topic Direct Instruction:

Part of learning and growing is knowing who you can talk to when things get confusing or hard. While oftentimes the person we go to first is our parent or guardian, there are other people who are important in our lives that we may also want to talk to about hard, confusing, or scary things. They might be a relative or family friend. They might be a community leader, like a priest, teacher, or coach. Having a trusted adult is important because it helps us feel safer and less alone. Having more than one trusted adult is nice because different situations in our lives may mean we go talk to different people.

So, what makes those other people a safe and trusted adult, and someone that we know is safe to talk to about anything? A trusted adult is someone that both you and your parents or guardians know and someone that will never ask you to keep a secret. They are someone that will listen to your worries and fears, and also your joys and excitement. They make you feel safe, respected, and accepted for who you are.

Activities:

- With your parent/guardian, write a list of every adult you can think of in your life and talk about ways you interact with them.
- From that big list, write a new list of 2-3 safe and trusted adults in your life, and make sure you share that list with your parent/guardian. Try to identify at least one adult you live with and one adult you don't in your list.
- Talk about in what kind of situations you might need to talk to your safe and trusted adult (ex: bullying, seeing something unfair, questions about puberty, questions about your personal identity, abuse, big accomplishments)

Reading Extensions:

- "How Could You? Kids Talk About Trust" by Nancy Loewen
- "The Itchy Secret" by Vicki Hamilton-Allen

Week 22 - Spiritual Connections: Important Myths 2

Weekly Routine:

☐ Key Topic
☐ Nature Observation
☐ Deity Focus
☐ Weekly Reflection

Key Topic Direct Instruction:

We talked about myths several weeks ago, and now we're going to spend some more time talking about it, because there are a LOT of myths.

Remember, there are a lot of categories of myths that you can read or hear about, and your family may not have a specific myth for each important thing, but that's okay. Some types of myths tell about the creation of the world, or how humans came to be. Some types of myths talk about the importance of hospitality and being nice to strangers. Some types of myths explain how we learned certain things (like how to make fire), or how we receive the blessings of the Gods. Some types of myths talk about fighting that happened between different groups of spirits or gods. Some types of myths tell the story of a hero and their adventures. Some types of myths talk about what happens after we die.

Activities:

- Read a myth that is important to your family. These will depend on what is available in your primary pantheon and what is important to your family. Possible options include:
    - Creation myths (humans, or the world in general)
    - Winning the waters/gaining wisdom myths
    - Myths that show importance of hospitality
    - Myths about a divine war
    - Myths about deities/spirits important to your family
    - Stories relating to the hero's cycle/monomyth
    - Stories about the afterlife
- Pick a myth that is new to your family and read it together.
- Draw a picture telling your favorite part of a myth you read or heard
- Retell or act out part of one of the myths you read or heard

- Talk about any lessons you might have learned from the myth you read or heard. Is there a certain way you should act or behave based on what that myth says?

Reading Extensions:
- "Treasury of Greek Mythology" by Donna Jo Napoli
- "Treasury of Norse Mythology" by Donna Jo Napoli
- "Celtic Mythology" by Philip Freeman
- "Myths, Legends, & Sacred Stories" by Philip Wilkinson
- "Celtic Mythology: History for Kids" by Dinobibi Publishing

Week 23 - How We Pray: Meditation & Trance

Weekly Routine:
- ☐ Key Topic
- ☐ Nature Observation
- ☐ Deity Focus
- ☐ Weekly Reflection

Key Topic Direct Instruction:

Meditation:

Meditation is one way that we can calm our body and mind. It helps us be more present in the moment, and it helps us focus on the thing we're trying to do. It's useful for us when we pray because a lot of times we can be distracted by the other things going on in our life. If we meditate, we can calm our body and mind, and focus on praying. A lot of meditation is being aware of yourself and where you are. This can include things like counting how long it takes you to breathe in and out, or naming all the things you can see around you.

Trance:

Trance is similar to meditation, because it takes place in our mind. While meditation can be done with your eyes open or closed, trance is often done by closing your eyes and allowing your mind and imagination to wander. One of the best ways to start to learn about trance is to do guided meditations.

Activities:

- Play 5,4,3,2,1 (5 things you can see, 4 things you can hear, 3 things you can touch, 2 things you can smell, 1 thing you can taste)
- Listen to a Guided Meditation
    - Three Cranes Meditations - https://threecranes.org/media/meditations/

Reading Extensions:

- "Moonbeam: A Book of Meditations for Children" by Maureen Garth (also her other books "Starbright", "Earthlight", and "Sunshine")
- "Breathe Like a Bear" by Kira Willey

Week 24 - Parts of Ritual: Grounding & Centering

Weekly Routine:

☐ Key Topic
☐ Nature Observation
☐ Deity Focus
☐ Weekly Reflection

Key Topic Direct Instruction:

We learned about meditation last week. This week we'll take that a step further and talk about grounding and centering, as well as a way to do both of those things.

What is Grounding?

Grounding is what you do when you have too much magical energy in your body. A lot of times this happens after you perform a ritual. When you feel like your body needs to move around after ritual, that can be a sign you need to ground. It's called grounding because you often direct all your extra energy into the ground, the same way that a lightning rod directs all the electricity from lightning into the ground.

What is Centering?

Centering is what you do to get ready for ritual, to help focus your mind and body on what you're getting ready to do. Meditation is one way that you can center yourself. When you center yourself, you gather energy from around you and bring it into yourself, and focus it into small point or ball within yourself. This focus makes it so you have energy to direct during the ritual. It makes you powerful and ready to do big or hard things.

The Two Powers

One way to ground and center yourself is called the Two Powers, which can be used in a type of guided meditation. Stand up really tall and reach your arms up over your head. Wiggle your toes into the ground. This is one way you can feel the Two Powers: the power of Sky and the power of Earth. They are opposites that work together to help us work magic. The Sky is bright and shining. The Earth is cool and dark.

When we do a Two Powers meditation, we are finding the center and power within ourselves. We start by feeling the Earth Power below us, and connecting to it. We imagine it filling our body. Then we go on to feel the Sky Power above us, and connect to it. We imagine it filling our body and touching the Earth Power already there. Then we imagine those two powers mixing in us and making us more centered and more powerful.

Then, when we need to ground, we again imagine ourselves as the Tree connecting the Earth and Sky, and send all the energy we've collected back into the Earth and Sky. When we're done, we have just the right amount of energy.

Activities:
- Listen to a Two Powers Meditation
    - Three Cranes Meditations - https://threecranes.org/media/meditations/
    - "A Toddler's Inner Grove Meditation" by Rev. Jan Avende - https://threecranes.org/wp-content/uploads/2018/05/Jan-Toddler-Inner-Grove.mp3
- Draw a picture or make a craft of the Two Powers connecting to you.
- Go outside and feel the earth under your feet, and feel the sun warming your body. Write or draw about this in your Kindling Sparks journal.

Reading Extensions:
- "Moonbeam: A Book of Meditations for Children" by Maureen Garth (also her other books "Starbright", "Earthlight", and "Sunshine")

Week 25 - High Day: Winter Cross Quarter

Weekly Routine:

☐ Key Topic
☐ Nature Observation
☐ Deity Focus
☐ Weekly Reflection

Key Topic Direct Instruction:

The winter cross quarter, often called Imbolc, is the time of year when the first signs of life are seen again, meaning that the winter is coming to a close and spring is just around the corner. Imbolc celebrates the fire that burns within, and the hearth. The deities that are honored at this time of year are often associated with the hearth and home, because that is where we're spending most of our time.

Just like how at Winter Solstice we noticed that it was time to stay inside more and spend time with family, that continues now. Ancient people would probably have stayed together around the hearth (like a fireplace) more in the deepest cold of wintertime.

Activities:

- Learn about traditions and deities that are associated with your family's primary pantheon(s)
- Learn about and look at pictures of animals (often lambs) that are symbolic of Imbolc
- Go for a nature walk and see if you can notice the very first signs of spring, like early bulb flowers
- Oats are a traditional food at Imbolc. Find a recipe with oats in it and make it with your adult helper.
- Make candle holders out of salt dough and decorate them for your altar.
- Make Brigid Crosses out of pipe cleaners (or rushes, for a more traditional craft)
- Perform a ritual for the Winter Cross Quarter
    - https://charteroakadf.org/family-resources/
    - Kindling Sparks Ritual Template (found in the back of the book)
- Use craft supplies to create a sun
- Listen to or read a story or myth about the Winter Cross Quarter

Reading Extensions:

- "Frederick" by Leo Lionni
- "The Snow Lambs" by Debi Gliori
- "Shanna and the Raven: an Imbolc Story" by Arie Farnam

- Note: there are many books about St. Brigid which may prove useful in telling some of her myths, but are told from a Christian point of view. One such book is "The Story of St. Brigid" by Caitriona Clarke

Week 26 - Our Virtues: Perseverance

Weekly Routine:

- ☐ Key Topic
- ☐ Nature Observation
- ☐ Deity Focus
- ☐ Weekly Reflection

Key Topic Direct Instruction:

Perseverance means that we don't give up, even when something is hard. Even if we fail at something, or mess something up, we try again and again until we succeed. It's important to remember that sometimes success means trying your best and trying not to be discouraged or upset when you fail. The important thing is to get back up, and do your best again.

Activities:

- Write or draw about a time you didn't succeed on the first try at something, but kept trying until you got it.
- Read a story about someone who overcame some obstacle in their life or in their projects. Scientists are great options.
- Do a project or practice a skill that you've been working on getting better at

Reading Extensions:

- "Perseverance: I Have Grit" by Jodie Shepherd
- "One More Time" by Nancy Loewen

- "Ada Twist, Scientist" by Andrea Beaty
- "Rosie Revere, Engineer" by Andrea Beaty
- "You Can Do It" by Craig Manning

Week 27 - Equality: Racial Equity & White Privilege

Weekly Routine:

☐ Key Topic
☐ Nature Observation
☐ Deity Focus
☐ Weekly Reflection

Key Topic Direct Instruction:

What is Equity?

Equity, which is similar to equality, is when people are treated in a way that gives them the same opportunities and quality of life no matter what they look like, where they come from, or what they can do. It means that we give each person, and each group of people, the tools they need to succeed. It isn't just giving everybody the exact same thing. If you broke your leg, and your friend has a cold, you wouldn't give your friend a cast just because you have one. They need something different than you to get better. When we have equity, that is being fair to everyone, because everyone has different needs.

What is White Privilege?

White privilege is when someone has more or better opportunities just because their skin is white. It doesn't mean their life is easy, but it means that they are treated differently because their skin is white, and don't have as many obstacles in their way. This privilege can be little things, like being able to easily find dolls in the store that have white skin, or seeing most of your favorite characters on tv have white skin. It can also be big things like someone who is white getting a job even though someone who is not white may be better at that job.

53

Or it could be someone who is not white being treated worse by the police or their teachers, and getting hurt for something a white person would be able to get away with.

How can I be an ally?

Being an ally means you stand up for people who have less privilege than you. You use your voice, your body, and your actions to help make sure they're treated in a way that helps them succeed and be safe, particularly if they're being treated unfairly because they're different. When someone is being treated unfairly, a good first step is to ask them if they're okay. Offer to stay with them while they feel hurt or unsafe. You can also be prepared to be an ally by identifying adults who are also allies ahead of time, so that if you need to get help you know who good people to go to are. One of the most important parts of being an ally is listening to the person you're trying to help. They may tell you something that would really help, or something you're doing that is not helping, and it's important to listen to and respect what they say.

Activities:

Caring Adult Support

- Add coloring supplies that allow children to show multiple skin tones
- Invest in dolls or other pretend play items that represent people who look different than you.
- Model being an ally and calling out injustice and microaggressions when you see them

Kid Activities

- Make a list of adults who are allies, and practice how you would ask them for help
- See if there is a pint-size, or kid-focused, protest group in your area, and attend a meeting or protest with them and your caring adult.
- Watch videos of a protest for equality with your caring adult, and talk about what the protestors want, and

why they needed to protest. Also talk about who at the protest is an ally
- Make a sign you could take to a protest
- Role play/pretend play how you would help someone who looks different than you if they were being treated unfairly.

Reading Extensions:

- *Caring Adult Book to help guide discussion:* "This Book is Anti-Racist" by Tiffany Jewell
- "On the Playground: Our First Talk about Prejudice" by Jillian Roberts
- "The Other Side" by Jacqueline Woodson
- "What Makes Us Unique: Our First Talk about Diversity" by Jillian Roberts
- "Not My Idea: A Book About Whiteness" by Anastasia Higginbotham
- "Let's Talk About Race" by Julius Lester
- "A Different Kind of Dragon" by Derek Nelson
- "You Are Mighty: A Guide to Changing the World" by Caroline Paul
- "Sulwe" by Lupita Nyong'o
- "The Proudest Blue: The Story of Hijab and Family" by Ibtihaj Muhammad
- "When We Were Alone" by David Robertson

Week 28 - Our Virtues: Fertility

Weekly Routine:

☐ Key Topic
☐ Nature Observation
☐ Deity Focus
☐ Weekly Reflection

Key Topic Direct Instruction:

Fertility is when you have potential to create. It is creativity, and the drive to make something new or different in your life. Sometimes we fall into routines where we always do the same things, play the same games, and color the same pictures. When we are practicing fertility, or creativity, we are focusing on what we can make that is new. We are engaging with our imagination. What kinds of things can you do to spark your creativity?

We can also engage in Fertility when we learn about growing things. Farmers talk about having fertile fields. This means that the field has the potential for good growth of crops.

Activities:

- Make a piece of art that uses different materials than normal (using natural materials, like sticks and leaves, is a great way to try something different)
- Visit a favorite playground and brainstorm what changes could be made to make it even more fun and exciting
- Grow a plant from seed. (beans make a great first plant to grow)
- During your nature observations for the week, notice what new things may be just starting to sprout or grow leaves. (snowdrops are pretty typical this time of year, and some trees may have buds starting)
- Visit the produce section of the grocery store and see if you can identify where different food comes from

Reading Extensions:

- "Journal Sparks" by Emily Neuburger
- "In My Room" by Jo Witek
- "Where's Your Creativity" by Aaron Rosen
- "What Will Grow" by Jennifer Ward
- "Farming" by Gail Gibbons

Week 29 - Parts of Ritual: Inspiration

Weekly Routine:

- ☐ Key Topic
- ☐ Nature Observation
- ☐ Deity Focus
- ☐ Weekly Reflection

Key Topic Direct Instruction:

Inspiration is something that we call for, or ask for, near the beginning of our rituals. This is because we want the words we say and the actions we do in ritual to come from the heart, and be meaningful. Inspiration is a thing that happens when we suddenly have a good idea or want to do something new or in a specific way. Sometimes when we pray, we use a script, and say the words that have already been written down, but sometimes when we pray, we speak whatever words come to mind. When we're speaking from the heart, and saying whatever comes to mind, we want those words to be understandable and meaningful, so we call for inspiration to help us. Sometimes we even call for a specific deity or spirit to help us be inspired, like Brigid, Oghma, Apollo, Odin, or the Awen.

Outside of ritual, inspiration leads to great discoveries and artworks. Scientists are inspired to try new methods, or have a great idea about how something might work. Poets and writers are inspired to create new works. Artists, dancers, and musicians let inspiration guide them when they are creative and making new works.

Activities:

- Say a prayer for inspiration before you make a craft or tell a story
- Learn to intone the Awen (https://www.philipcarr-gomm.com/awen/)

Reading Extensions:
- "What Do You Do With An Idea" by Kobi Yamada
- "Leonardo Da Vinci" by Francesca Romei
- "Before the World was Ready" by Claire Eamer
- "Fancy Nancy: Poet Extraordinaire!" by Jane O'Connor

Week 30 - How We Pray: Magic

Weekly Routine:

☐ Key Topic
☐ Nature Observation
☐ Deity Focus
☐ Weekly Reflection

Key Topic Direct Instruction:

When we think of magic, we often think of wand waving to create fantastic effects or potion brewing to make potent elixirs. These fantasy visions of magic are pretty different from what magic looks like in our religion. For us, magic is more subtle. It is a combination of setting intentions (what do we want to happen), and taking actions to help make that happen. Some common types of magic involve color correspondence, candles, herbs, crystals, songs, or spoken charms.

Activities:

- Look up some color correspondences, and pick a goal you want to achieve. Then choose a candle of that color and light it while you think about your goal. Let it burn for a little bit, then snuff or blow it out.
- Choose some protective crystals or herbs and set them up around the edges or corners of your room
- Make up a rhyming phrase to focus on a goal you want to achieve

Reading Extensions:
- "Look to the Moon" by J. C. Artemisia
- "A Kid's Herb Book" by Leslie Tierra
- "What is Magic?" by Rowen Moss

Week 31 - Key Spirits: Shining Ones

Weekly Routine:

☐ Key Topic
☐ Nature Observation
☐ Deity Focus
☐ Weekly Reflection

Key Topic Direct Instruction:

The Shining Ones refers to the deities, the Gods, Goddesses, and Godden (deities that are neither male nor female). While they may not all "shine," they do all radiate power. The Shining Ones each have a specialty that allows them to connect to each other and/or the world we live in. There are those who work in the Upper Realm, like deities of the sky, air, sun, wind and storm. There are those who work in the mid-realm, like deities of the forest, hearth, money, war, and crafts. There are those who work in the Underworld, deities of death, and wealth.

Activities:
- Build a shrine to a specific deity
- Draw a picture of a specific deity
- Make a toilet paper roll icon from Werkelwald, or of your own creation
    - Toilet Paper Roll Deity Images (by Birgit Reinhartz): http://werkelwald.de/etwas-respektlos-aber-dennoch-klorollengoetter/

(website is in German, but downloads for the pictures are easy to find)

Reading Extension:

- "Z is for Zeus" by Helen L Wilbur - simple ABC book for main storyline, with in depth descriptions for each thing on each page.
    - "The Kindreds" by Rev. Kathleen Pezza
        - https://www.lulu.com/en/us/shop/rev-kathleen-pezza/the-kindred/paperback/product-17ge67e8.html

Week 32 - High Day: Spring Equinox

Weekly Routine:

☐ Key Topic
☐ Nature Observation
☐ Deity Focus
☐ Weekly Reflection

Key Topic Direct Instruction:

Spring Equinox, often called Ostara, is the time of year when winter is finally letting go of the world and the day and night are the same length. It is a time for fertility, new life, and new beginnings. Farmers can begin planting, and new livestock are born to sustain the herds. We focus on perseverance and renewal in particular during this rite because historically this is the leanest part of the year. The food stores from winter were running low, but the new crops hadn't begun growing yet. We also focus on balance, because the day and night are the same length.

Activities:

- Learn about traditions and deities that are associated with your family's primary pantheon(s)
- Go for a nature walk and see what you can notice in nature that happens at spring time, like buds and new leaves on trees, baby animals, and some flowers
- Use craft supplies to create flowers
- Listen to or read a story or myth about the Spring Equinox
- Read about the scientific meanings of the Spring Equinox
- Start some plants indoors so you can watch them grow. Bunching onions and radishes are good choices this time of year.
- Decorate eggs
- Decorate your house and/or altar with signs of spring (bouquets of flowers are a great option)
- Do a spring cleaning of at least one room in your house, then invite the spirits back into this new clean space
- Make a list of goals for the coming season (new projects you want to start, or interpersonal qualities you want to work on)
- Perform a ritual for the Spring Equinox
    - https://charteroakadf.org/family-resources/
    - Kindling Sparks Ritual Template (found in the back of the book)

Reading Extensions:

- "The Spring Equinox" by Ellen Jackson
- "A New Beginning" by Wendy Pfeffer
- "Happy Springtime" by Kate McMullan

Week 33 - Our Virtues: Wisdom

Weekly Routine:

☐ Key Topic
☐ Nature Observation
☐ Deity Focus
☐ Weekly Reflection

Key Topic Direct Instruction:

Wisdom is a virtue that means you take your time to think about things before taking action. Someone who is wise is often someone who is deliberate about their choices, and focuses on doing the best they can with the situation they are presented with.

Activities:

- Think of someone you know who you consider "wise". Why do you think they're wise?
- Write or draw about what wisdom, or being wise, looks like
- Learn about a deity who is wise
- Write or draw about a time you made good choices

Reading Extensions:

- "Wisdom Stories" by Mary Joslin
- "Aesop's Fables" (various authors)

Week 34 - Parts of Ritual: Divination & Omens

Weekly Routine:

☐ Key Topic
☐ Nature Observation

- ☐ Deity Focus
- ☐ Weekly Reflection

Key Topic Direct Instruction:

What is divination?

Divination is seeking guidance or answers from the spirits about a specific situation. It often means looking at the future to seek what options await us based on our past actions. Divination is also a main way that we can communicate with the spirits. It is a way for us to ask questions of them about their likes and dislikes, as well as ask for advice about specific things. Divination is often done with a symbol set of some variety. This is commonly done through alphabetic symbols or cards with elaborate pictures on them. Each symbol or card has a specific meaning. The diviner, or seer, will ask a question and then look to the symbol or card and interpret it to answer the question they asked.

What is the Omen?

The Omen is a specific part of a full ritual. It is the point of communication between us and the spirits. At this point in the ritual, we can learn if the spirits have liked our gifts and we can see what gifts they might offer us in return.

Activities:

- Get out a letter-based symbol set and draw pictures representing what each symbol means (looking up meanings is perfectly okay)
- Get out a card-based symbol set and try to pick out and share as many details about the picture that you can see.
- Go outside and look around. Think about what words you associate with certain things in nature (ex: song birds, birds of prey, squirrels, flowers, specific trees, clouds, rocks, etc.)

Reading Extensions:
- Look for books about the specific symbol set you're wanting to learn more about.

Week 35 - Environment: Sustainability & Conservation

Weekly Routine:

☐ Key Topic
☐ Nature Observation
☐ Deity Focus
☐ Weekly Reflection

Key Topic Direct Instruction:

Sustainability is making sure that when we use something, we don't use so much that there is not enough left for people to use it in the future. We need sustainable resources to be able to create a better world for the future. Sustainability is about more than us, it's about kids in the future being able to also live happy and healthy lives because we were careful with our resources.

Conservation means protecting things, like plants and animals, that are in danger because of the effect humans have on the environment. Conservation happens when we think about how our actions will affect others and the world around us, and move to protect them.

It is important to focus not only on the things we can do personally to be sustainable in our living and protect the environment, but also on the larger things the world can do to help preserve our natural resources, the plant and animal life, and the Earth as a whole.

Activities:
- Brainstorm a list of things you can do to be sustainable in your home, and then pick a few to focus on doing
- Visit a zoo and learn about animals who have lost, or are losing, their habitats
- Visit a nature preserve, local or state park, or botanical garden and learn about plants that are threatened by human activity

Reading Extensions:
- "Sustainable Living" by Harriet Brundle
- "Go Green with Greta" by Eliza Brookfield
- "If You Take Away the Otter" by Susannah Burhman-Deever
- "The Lorax" by Dr. Seuss
- "Making a City Sustainable" by Courtney Farrell

Week 36 - Our Virtues: Integrity

Weekly Routine:

☐ Key Topic
☐ Nature Observation
☐ Deity Focus
☐ Weekly Reflection

Key Topic Direct Instruction:

Integrity is a virtue that means we are both true to ourselves, but also true to our word. When we are acting in a way that is full of integrity, we are being honest, loyal, fair, and self-confident. Integrity is important to being a good friend, and important to feeling good about yourself.

Activities:

- Draw a picture or write about the things that make you special
- Write a list of the things you are good at and like doing
- Make a list of people who you think demonstrate integrity
- Do a random act of kindness

Reading Extensions:

- "Teach Your Dragon to Stop Lying" by Steve Herman
- "Honesty" by Kelli Hicks
- "The 'I' in Integrity" by Julia Cook
- "Stand Tall" by Cheri J. Meiners

Week 37 - High Day: Spring Cross Quarter

Weekly Routine:

- ☐ Key Topic
- ☐ Nature Observation
- ☐ Deity Focus
- ☐ Weekly Reflection

Key Topic Direct Instruction:

The spring cross quarter, often called Beltane, is a time of revelry, and similar to Samhain, is a time when the veil between the worlds is thin. It is another liminal, or in-between, time. It is often considered a time when the fairies and other Nature Spirits are very present in our world. Because of this it is seen as a time when we can communicate more easily with the deities and Nature Spirits.

Some common ideas around this time are celebrating colors, flowers, new life, and love. It is a time when we can focus on the bright beauty of the world, and celebrate creativity and fertility of the land around us. One tradition that is common for this High Day is dancing the May Pole. This is a tall pole that you attach many different colored ribbons to, and then weave them around the pole as you dance with others. Another common tradition is to have a bonfire and either dance around it, or walk between two bonfires that are close to each other. This also helps us celebrate the joy of the season, the many kinds of love that there are, and the fertility of the land.

Activities:
- Make a flower crown
- Build and dance around a may pole
- Watch a video of Morris dancers
- Dance around a campfire
- Build a fairy garden
- Decorate your altar with flowers
- Collect flowers for a spring bouquet
- Host a drum circle
- Paint smooth rocks with nature and fire symbols to set out in your garden
- Perform a ritual for the Spring Cross Quarter
    - https://charteroakadf.org/family-resources/
    - Kindling Sparks Ritual Template (found in the back of the book)

Reading Extensions:
- "The Rainbow Tulip" by Pat Mora
- "On the Morn of Mayfest" by Erica Silverman
- "Shanna and the Water Fairy" by Ari Farnam
- "What Makes a Rainbow" by Betty Ann Schwartz

Week 38 - A Diverse World: Indigenous Religions

Weekly Routine:

☐ Key Topic

- ☐ Nature Observation
- ☐ Deity Focus
- ☐ Weekly Reflection

Key Topic Direct Instruction:

Indigenous religions are the religious and cultural beliefs of the people who lived here before us, and in some cases these people still live around us. In North America, these are the beliefs of the Native Americans and First Nations people. It's important to remember that not all Indigenous tribes are the same, and they all have unique and beautiful traditions and languages that are specific to them. While the beliefs and myths vary by tribe, many have some focus on the sacredness of the Earth and reverence for nature. One other thing we need to remember is to acknowledge that we are living on land that used to belong to these indigenous peoples.

Activities:

- Learn the names of the different tribes that lived, and live, near you
- Visit a historical Indigenous site near you
- Find street and city names that come from your local Indigenous tribe's language
- Read an Indigenous myth
- Learn the Indigenous names for landmarks near you
- Read land acknowledgements from various groups and governments

Reading Extensions:

- Research about tribes local to your location.
    - North America: https://native-land.ca
- "We Are Water Protectors" by Carol Lindstrom
- "We Are Grateful; Otsaliheliga" by Traci Sorell
- "All Around Us" by Xelene Gonzalez
- "Rabbit's Snow Dance" by James Bruchac
- "Tasunka" by Donald F. Montileaux
- "Lessons From Mother Earth" by Elaine Mcleod

Week 39 - Equality: Cultural Appropriation

Weekly Routine:

☐ Key Topic
☐ Nature Observation
☐ Deity Focus
☐ Weekly Reflection

Key Topic Direct Instruction:

Cultural appropriation means that we can't do things from another culture in a way that is disrespectful to those other cultures. This is especially true for cultures that have been colonized, or forcefully influenced, by non-native people, like indigenous groups. It can be disrespectful to wear traditional clothes, especially as a costume, or do religious rituals from a culture that is not your own.

There is a difference between appropriation and appreciation. Appropriation is like stealing. It is something that is done without permission. Appreciation is something that we do with permission and in a way that is respectful and celebrating another culture. Some cultures are very protective of their traditional dress, religious practices, and lifestyle because they've had it taken from them so many times. It is their right to decide that no one else is allowed to use or do those things. It's like the difference between someone copying your work in school, and you working in a group to learn together.

Activities:

- Attend a multicultural festival
- Support a minority owned business
- Learn a few phrases from an endangered language
- Read a book by an Indigenous author
- Look at, and talk about, a piece of art by a native artist

- Learn about a living or historical famous person from an Indigenous culture
- Cook a meal from an Indigenous culture

Reading Extensions:

- "My Food, Your Food, Our Food" by Emma Carlson Berne
- "Food Like Mine" part of the DK Children Just Like Me series
- "Explore Native American Cultures" by Anita Yasuda
- "Fry Bread" by Kevin Noble Maillard

Week 40 - Key Spirits: Nature Spirits

Weekly Routine:

☐ Key Topic
☐ Nature Observation
☐ Deity Focus
☐ Weekly Reflection

Key Topic Direct Instruction:

The Nature Spirits can be divided into two broad categories: those beings of nature that we can see, and those we can't. The first type of Nature Spirit is the more obvious. They are the creatures that live in our world: the birds, fish, insects, reptiles and mammals, but they are also the trees, rivers, rocks, plants, dirt, and oceans. They are all part of the ecosystem that makes our world work together and function.

The second type of Nature Spirit, the kind you can't see, are the mythical creatures. This incorporates creatures that live hidden in our world or are described in myths, like nymphs and dryads, fairies, spirits of the local land, and house spirits. They can also be creatures that take on roles beyond that of their real-world counterparts, like an animal that lives in the spirit world and represents all animals of that species.

Activities:

- Build a fairy house or fairy garden outside
- Write or draw about a Nature Spirit that is important to you
- Visit a local zoo, conservatory, or botanical garden
- Start a rock collection
- Plant trees or flowers, or work in your garden
- Put up a bird feeder in your yard
- Go on a hike and observe what aspects of nature and the ecosystem you see

Reading Extensions:

- "The Kindreds" by Rev. Kathleen Pezza
    - https://www.lulu.com/en/us/shop/rev-kathleen-pezza/the-kindred/paperback/product-17ge67e8.html
- "Under the Same Sky" by Britta Teckentrup
- "You Are Stardust" by Elin Kelsey
- "You Are Never Alone" by Elin Kelsey

Week 41 - Consent & The Self: Bodily Autonomy

Weekly Routine:

- ☐ Key Topic
- ☐ Nature Observation
- ☐ Deity Focus
- ☐ Weekly Reflection

Key Topic Direct Instruction:

Bodily autonomy, or personal sovereignty, means that we each get to decide what happens to our own body, without someone else trying to tell us what to do. Sovereignty means being in charge. Each person is in charge of their own body. That means that you have the responsibility to take good care of your body and that you have the right to decide what happens to your body. When you're interacting with other people this can be things as simple as making sure you have permission to give them a hug. Additionally, if someone asks if they can give you a hug, you can say no. You can always say no when someone asks to touch your body, even if they are adults. It is always your choice what happens to your body.

You also get to decide how much personal space you want. This is like a bubble that surrounds you. Other people need to ask before they come into your bubble, and you need to ask before going into someone else's bubble. Not everyone's bubble is the same size, and that's okay. It's about what each person is comfortable with.

Activities:

- Roleplay with your caring adult interactions where you agree to a wave, handshake, or hug as a greeting or goodbye. Practice verbally saying yes and no.
- Learn about anatomy, and the difference between different people's bodies, with your caring adult
- Draw a picture of you in your bubble, and add in the things that are okay in your bubble and the things that aren't

Reading Extensions:

- "Consent (for Kids!)" by Rachel Brian
- "No Means No!" by Jayneen Sanders
- "My Body! What I Say Goes!" by Jayneen Sanders
- "Let's Talk About Body Boundaries, Consent, and Respect" by Jayneen Sanders
- "Don't Touch My Hair" by Sharee Miller

Week 42 - Our Virtues: Moderation

Weekly Routine:

☐ Key Topic
☐ Nature Observation
☐ Deity Focus
☐ Weekly Reflection

Key Topic Direct Instruction:

Moderation is when we don't do too much of something, but we don't do too little either. It's about finding a balance with the things in our life. This can be everything from how much sleep we get, to how much we eat of each thing, to how much glue we use in a craft project.

Activities:

- Taste a food when you add too much salt to it (like potatoes or eggs), or when you add too little sugar (like unsweetened baking chocolate) and write or draw about the experience
- Make a picture collage of your favorite things, being careful to use just the right amount of liquid glue

Reading Extensions:

- "Goldilocks and the Three Bears" by Jan Brett (there are many versions of this story, so pick one that's accessible for you)
- "Just Add Glitter" by Angela DiTerlizzi

Week 43 - Consent & The Self: Knowing & Caring For Me

Weekly Routine:

☐ Key Topic
☐ Nature Observation
☐ Deity Focus
☐ Weekly Reflection

Key Topic Direct Instruction:

There are lots of ways that we can take care of and love ourselves. We need to take care of our emotional needs and respect how we see ourselves (our identity). This can include things like learning about and respecting our gender identity and improving our self-esteem. We need to take care of our physical needs and how we take care of our body. This includes things like good hygiene (brushing teeth, taking baths, washing hands, etc.), eating well, and exercise. We need to take care of our mental needs and make sure we're able to give our best effort. This includes things like learning coping skills for when we're nervous or anxious about something, getting good sleep, and eating well.

Activities:

- Make a handwashing poster to hang in your bathroom showing all the correct steps for good handwashing
- Perform the "How Clean Are Your Hands" bread experiment from C.S. Mott Children's Hospital (https://www.mottchildren.org/posts/camp-little-victors/dirty-hands)
- Learn about different pronouns that people use to refer to themselves (feminine, masculine, non-binary, etc.)
- Learn about the difference between sex and gender with your caring adult
- Learn about and fill out the Gender Unicorn for you (https://transstudent.org/gender/)

- Create some positive affirmations that you can say to yourself in the morning
- Plan and cook a well-rounded meal for your family

Reading Extensions:

- "Neither" by Airlie Anderson
- "Julian is a Mermaid" by Jessica Love
- "Listening to My Body" by Gabi Garcia
- "Teach Your Dragon Good Hygiene" by Steve Herman
- "Tell me about Sex, Grandma" by Anastasia Higginbotham

Week 44 - Spiritual Connections: Ancient History

Weekly Routine:

☐ Key Topic
☐ Nature Observation
☐ Deity Focus
☐ Weekly Reflection

Key Topic Direct Instruction:

A lot of our information about our beliefs comes from knowing what ancient people believed, and how they lived. When we study how ancient people live, we learn the types of things that were important to them. For example, being able to grow food so that you can eat and feed your livestock was very important, so it makes sense that the ancient people believed in gods of agriculture (or farming). Learning about their lives also lets us look at how our lives are the same and different. When we see how our lives are the same, we can understand the deities that we worship a bit better.

Activities:
- Learn about a family tradition and talk about how it came to be a tradition in your family
- Talk to your caring adult and learn what technology they didn't have that you do, and how they managed without it
- Pretend a room in your house is discovered by some future civilization. Write or draw about the items they might find, and what they may think they'd be used for
- Create an item out of craft supplies that might be found in an ancient culture (ex: mask, vase, clothing, weapon, tool, ship or cart, etc.)
- Read about a famous person from an ancient culture
- Watch a video about an ancient people
- Visit a museum that has an ancient civilization exhibit
- Build an ancient building using craft supplies or natural materials

Reading Extensions:
- "Ancient Greece" by Anne Pearson
- "The Scandinavian Vikings" by Louise Park
- "Ancient Rome" by Simon James
- "Life of the Ancient Celts" by Hazel Richardson

Week 45 - High Day: Summer Solstice

Weekly Routine:

☐ Key Topic
☐ Nature Observation
☐ Deity Focus
☐ Weekly Reflection

Key Topic Direct Instruction:

Summer Solstice, often called Midsummer or Litha, is the longest day of the year. It is a time to celebrate the glory and power of the sun, as well as the mighty Fire within ourselves. During this celebration there are often many bonfires or other things symbolizing the fire. The Summer Solstice is not just a religious holiday, it is also an astrological event, when the Earth is tilted towards the sun, making our days longer and warmer.

Activities:

- Make a craft about the Sun
- Make a suncatcher
- Make a sundial
- Play outside
- Watch a video of the sunrise over Stonehenge
- Make and wear a flower wreath or flower crown
- Learn about deities of the Sun (ex: Helios, Sunna, Sol Invictus, Saulé, Belenos, etc.)
- Make of list of things you want to do or accomplish this coming year
- Wake up with the dawn and light a candle welcoming in the Sun
- Stay up late with a campfire
- Perform a ritual for the Summer Solstice
    - https://charteroakadf.org/family-resources/
    - Kindling Sparks Ritual Template (found in the back of the book)

Reading Extensions:

- "The Longest Day: Celebrating the Summer Solstice" by Wendy Pfeffer
- "Summer Solstice" by Maddie Spalding
- "The Summer Solstice" by Ellen Jackson

Week 46 - Spiritual Connections: The Wide Variety of Cultural Hearths

Weekly Routine:

- ☐ Key Topic
- ☐ Nature Observation
- ☐ Deity Focus
- ☐ Weekly Reflection

Key Topic Direct Instruction:

We've learned about deities from multiple pantheons (or groups of deities based on culture). A cultural hearth is one way to look at both the pantheon (or deities) and the ancient historical practices together. When you worship deities that all come from the same pantheon you're worshipping within a cultural hearth. There is no reason you have to worship deities from the same pantheon, and many people are drawn to a wide variety of deities and spirits from across cultures. Some examples of cultural hearths are Irish, Norse, Hellenic, Roman, Gaulish, and Slavic. When we look at the culture and the pantheon together, we can see ways that the culture influenced the way the deities acted, and how the myths help tell stories that were important to the individual culture.

Activities:

- Write a story or draw a picture of people and deities interacting with each other
- Read about an ancient culture's religion

Reading Extensions:

- "Myths, Legends, & Sacred Stories" by Philip Wilkinson
- "Ancient Greece" by Anne Pearson
- "The Scandinavian Vikings" by Louise Park
- "Myths & Legends of Ancient Britain and Ireland" by Scott A. Leonard

Week 47 - Key Spirits: Patrons & Allies

Weekly Routine:

- ☐ Key Topic
- ☐ Nature Observation
- ☐ Deity Focus
- ☐ Weekly Reflection

Key Topic Direct Instruction:

In paganism it is fairly common to have deities or spirits who are special to you, and who feel a deep connection to. They may take a particular interest in you, or you may like to do the same things that they like to do. These deities or spirits are our allies, and are often called Patrons. A Patron is someone who is more powerful than you, but who cares for you. You build a relationship based on hospitality, but understand that they will always be able to give you more than you can give them. Some people have just one Patron, some people have many, and some people have none. All of these are okay.

It's common to have special prayers or special offerings that you give to your Patron. These can be things like plants that are special to them, poetry you've written for them, or pictures you've drawn for them. These offerings come from the heart and are a way for you to show your special love and relationship with this deity or spirit.

Activities:

- Research deities that have similar interests to you, and make an offering to them
- Build a shrine to a Patron
- Make a toilet paper roll icon from Werkelwald, or of your own creation
    - Toilet Paper Roll Deity Images (by Birgit Reinhartz): http://werkelwald.de/etwas-respektlos-aber-dennoch-klorollengoetter/

(website is in German, but downloads for the pictures are easy to find)

Reading Extensions:
- "Treasury of Greek Mythology" by Donna Jo Napoli
- "Treasury of Norse Mythology" by Donna Jo Napoli
- "Celtic Mythology" by Philip Freeman
- "Myths, Legends, & Sacred Stories" by Philip Wilkinson
- "Celtic Mythology: History for Kids" by Dinobibi Publishing

Week 48 - A Diverse World: Monotheistic Religions

Weekly Routine:

- ☐ Key Topic
- ☐ Nature Observation
- ☐ Deity Focus
- ☐ Weekly Reflection

Key Topic Direct Instruction:

Monotheistic religions believe that there is only one god, or divine being. That's what "mono" means: one. This is different from polytheistic religions, which believe there are many gods, and atheism, which believes there are no gods. Oftentimes monotheistic religions believe that this one god sees and knows everything. Monotheistic religions often have a book that contains sacred texts. These readings help the worshipers of these religions define and practice their beliefs. Some of the large world religions that are monotheistic are Islam, Christianity, and Judaism.

Activities:
- Visit a place of monotheistic place of worship with your caring adult

- Read a myth or excerpt from a monotheistic sacred text

Reading Extensions:
- "What You Will See Inside a Mosque" by Aisha Karen Khan
- "Who Was Jesus?" by Ellen Morgan
- "Judaism" by Adam Lewinsky
- "Christianity" by Aaron Bowen
- "Islam" by Michael Ashkar

Week 49 - A Diverse World: Polytheistic Religions

Weekly Routine:

☐ Key Topic
☐ Nature Observation
☐ Deity Focus
☐ Weekly Reflection

Key Topic Direct Instruction:

Polytheistic religions believe that there are many gods and spirits in the world. "Poly" means "many". This is different for the monotheistic religions we learned about last week, which believe there is only one god. We are a polytheistic religion, and believe there are lots of gods and spirits. Our deities are limited, which means that they don't see or know everything, and they have specific things to focus their attention and expertise on. We draw our knowledge of the deities from both ancient texts, like myths and hymns, and personal experience. Paganism comes in many types, including Druidry, Wicca, Asatru, Eclectic Witchcraft, Hellenic Reconstructionism, Devotional Polytheism, and many others. Besides paganism, some other polytheistic religions are Hinduism and Shinto.

Activities:
- Visit a place of polytheistic worship other than your own with your caring adult
- Read a myth from a polytheistic religion other than one from your own beliefs

Reading Extensions:
- "Hinduism" by Harriet Brundle
- "Hinduism" by Nalini Rangan
- "Shinto" by Stuart A Kallen
- "Shinto" by Paula Hartz
- "Who is a Witch?" by Rowen Moss
- "The Charge of the Goddess" by Doreen Valiente (http://www.doreenvaliente.com/Doreen-Valiente-Doreen_Valiente_Poetry-11.php)

Week 50 - Our Virtues: Vision

Weekly Routine:

☐ Key Topic
☐ Nature Observation
☐ Deity Focus
☐ Weekly Reflection

Key Topic Direct Instruction:

Vision is the ability to broaden your perspective in order to see where you fit in the world and cosmos. The ways you learn about where you stand are from the past, the present, and what you think you'll grow into in the future. Oftentimes when we think about what would make the world a better place, full of tolerance, justice, and equity, we are embodying the virtue of vision. Vision is all about looking for a brighter future.

Activities:
- Make a list of wishes you have for the world
- Make a list of actions that you can take to make the world a better place, then do one of them
- Read a story about a person, character, or deity that you think exhibits Vision

Reading Extensions:
- "What We'll Build" by Oliver Jeffers
- "Oh, the Places You'll Go!" by Dr. Seuss

Week 51 - A Diverse World: An Interfaith Community

Weekly Routine:

☐ Key Topic
☐ Nature Observation
☐ Deity Focus
☐ Weekly Reflection

Key Topic Direct Instruction:

One of the things that makes the world beautiful is an acceptance of others who believe differently than us. When we gather with people who have different beliefs, we are becoming part of an interfaith community. This means that we can share our beliefs without trying to make others believe the same way we do, and can instead appreciate the shared and beautiful aspects of each of our individual faiths.

Activities:
- Visit an interfaith meeting or service with your caring adult

- Host or attend a multicultural playdate
- Attend a multicultural festival in your area
- Research what virtues are common amongst many religions, especially in regards to how we treat others
- Learn about different rites of passage in a variety of religions (ex: bar/bat mitzvah, baptism, namkaran, baby blessing, handfasting, etc.)

Reading Extensions:

- "My Religion, Your Religion" by Lisa Bullard
- "Empathy is Your Superpower" by Cori Bussolari
- "Hats of Faith" by Medeia Cohan

Week 52 - High Day: Summer Cross Quarter

Weekly Routine:

- ☐ Key Topic
- ☐ Nature Observation
- ☐ Deity Focus
- ☐ Weekly Reflection

Key Topic Direct Instruction:

The summer cross quarter, often called Lughnasadh or Lammas, is the first of the three harvest festivals. The summer months where food is in short supply due to the heat are coming to an end and the bounty of the fall harvests is a time for celebration. This is also a time when many cultures would hold a festival, often containing games of strength and skill.

Activities:

- Watch recordings of the Summer Olympics
- Attend a county or state fair

- Research what early harvest crops are in your area (often forms of grain and/or berries), and make a food using those ingredients
- Play backyard games with your friends & family (ex: horseshoes, sack races, tug of war, lawn bowling, croquet, bocce ball, etc.)
- Make a corn dollie (out of corn husks, yarn, pipe cleaners, etc.), or another wheat weaving project
- Go berry picking
- Perform a ritual for the Summer Cross Quarter
    - https://charteroakadf.org/family-resources/
    - Kindling Sparks Ritual Template

Reading Extensions:

- "The Coming of Lugh" from Celtic Wonder Tales - https://www.sacred-texts.com/neu/celt/cwt/cwt07.htm
- "The Tale of John Barleycorn" by Mary Azarian
- "Olympics" by Richard Platt

Weekly Routine Worksheet

Date: _____

☐ Key Topic: _____

This is the special topic that changes each week. Follow your child's lead if they'd like to write or draw about something from the week. Choose something from the Activities section to do, and something to read from the Reading Extensions.

☐ Nature Observation

Make time at least once each week to get outside and do some nature observation. Write or draw in your Nature Journal about what you see. Try sketching the distinguishing features of the plants or animals. Here's some notes to get you started:

- Where did we go: _____
  _____

- The weather was: _____
  _____

- I saw these animals: _____
  _____

- I saw these plants: _____
  _____

☐ Deity Focus: _____

Each week you will choose a different deity to focus on and learn about. Follow your child's lead about what they might be interested in, and look for deities that align with that interest. You should also make sure to include deities that are important to your family.

☐ Weekly Reflection

In their journal, encourage your child to respond in their own way on how they've incorporated paganism into their life this week. Some good questions to answer are "How have I embodied hospitality this week?" and "How have I been a good steward of the earth this week?" Feel free to add your own questions as well.

(You can print this page at: https://tinyurl.com/WeeklyRoutine)

Key Topics By Category (Unit Studies)

Rather than following the week-by-week order of Key Topics, some families may want to group these topics together by larger category. The provided tables here will allow you to jump to the appropriate weeks within each category, and the categories can be completed in any order. If you decide to work the Key Topics as Unit Studies, be sure to continue with the Weekly Routine activities as well.

High Days (8 topics)

Autumn Equinox (week 6)
Autumn Cross Quarter (week 11)
Winter Solstice (week 19)
Winter Cross Quarter (week 25)
Spring Equinox (week 32)
Spring Cross Quarter (week 37)
Summer Solstice (week 45)
Summer Cross Quarter (week 51)

Our Virtues (9 topics)

Hospitality (week 1)
Piety (week 7)

Courage (week 17)
Perseverance (week 26)
Fertility (week 28)
Wisdom (week 33)
Integrity (week 36)
Moderation (week 42)
Vision (week 50)

Spiritual Connections (5 topics)

The Spirits Our Family Honors (week 5)
Important Myths 1 (week 15)
Important Myths 2 (week 22)
Ancient History (week 44)
The Wide Variety of Cultural Hearths (week 46)

Key Spirits (6 topics)

The Earth Mother & Loving the Earth (week 3)

Liminal Spirits (week 10)
Ancestors (week 20)
Shining Ones (week 31)
Nature Spirits (week 40)
Patrons & Allies (week 47)

How We Pray (5 topics)

Service (week 4)
Devotionals & Prayer (week 8)
Ritual (week 12)
Meditation & Trance (week 23)
Magic (week 30)

Parts of Ritual (6 topics)

Sacred Center & Gates (week 9)
Return Flow (week 14)
Purification (week 16)

Grounding & Centering (week 24)
Inspiration (week 29)
Divination & Omens (week 34)

Consent & The Self (4 topics)

Healthy Relationships (week 2)
Trusted Adults (week 21)
Bodily Autonomy (week 41)
Knowing & Caring for Me (week 43)

Equality (3 topics)

Understanding Fairness (week 18)
Racial Equality & White Privilege (week 27)
Cultural Appropriation (week 39)

A Diverse World (4 topics)

Indigenous Religions (week 38)
Monotheistic Religions (week 48)
Polytheistic Religions (week 49)
An Interfaith Community (week 52)

Environment (2 topics)

Cycles & Seasons (week 13)
Sustainability (week 35)

Kindling Sparks High Day Template

Notes:

For this rite you'll pick your Being of the Occasion to match the season. During the key offerings you'll describe and maybe tell a story about that Being, and then make some offerings for them. Consider focusing your weekly deity study on a spirit that matches the seasonal celebration. This would be a great opportunity to do a craft project that can be the main offering to the Being of the Occasion.

Feel free to adapt this ritual to meet the needs of your child. You may find it best to shorten or lengthen parts based on their attention span. There are many opportunities to make offerings to the individual spirits throughout the ritual. These are optional, but are a great way to keep kids engaged. Additionally, there are suggested songs throughout the ritual. Feel free to change or add to the songs you use, particularly if you also practice with a group that uses specific songs.

You will need:

- Fire, or child-safe representation of fire
- Well
- Tree (or culturally appropriate alternative)
- Special offering for the Being of the Occasion (craft opportunity)
- Offerings for the other spirits (x4) - optional

The Script

Introduction

Today we are going to do a ritual to honor [spirit] for the [holiday]. We're going to invite all their friends and throw them a big ritual party. We will get to bring them gifts, and then we'll share [food and drink (Return Flow)] at the end of the ritual party.

Processional

Now it's time for us to go to our ritual space where we have our altar set up.

(to the tune of Farmer in the Dell)
We're going to the grove!
We're going to the grove!
We'll honor all the spirits!
We're going to the grove!

Purification

It's important for us to have ready minds and bodies before we honor the Spirits. Think of all the things that might make it hard for you to pay attention while we pray today. Imagine them on your skin and then let's brush them off together.

optional: sing "Shoo Fly" or "Shake Your Sillies Out"

Honoring the Earth Mother

Earth Mother, you are beautiful in all your seasons,
You care for us and provide for us.
Earth Mother, we honor you!

Inspiration

Now because we want our words, actions, and offerings to make the spirits happy we're going to ask for some inspiration by singing the word "Awen" three times.
"Aaa oooo ennn
Aaa oooo ennn
Aaa oooo ennn"

Attunement

As we get ready to make this place sacred, let's connect ourselves to the world around us. Our roots stretch down into the earth, our branches reach high into the sky, and a fire burns in our heart. Let's stretch our bodies out like a tree and breathe deeply three times.

Recreate the Cosmos

Now we're going to establish our Hallows so that we're ready to pray. We light the Fire and hallow the Well so that our prayers can be heard. We call on the Tree to send our voices across the realms.

Sing adapted verses for "My Roots Go Down"

My roots go down, down to the earth,
My roots go down, down to the earth,
My roots go down, down to the earth,
My roots go down.

1) I am a fire bright and strong
2) I am a well dark and deep
3) I am a tree connecting all

Opening the Gates

We now call out to our Gatekeeper to hold open the gates so that we can speak more easily to the Spirits. Gatekeeper, [or specific spirit], be with us as we get ready to pray. Let our Fire open as a gate. Let our Well open as a gate. Let our Tree connect all the realms and open as a gate.

Let the Gates be Open!

Honoring the Ancestors

Ancestors, you lived before us. Thank you for the love and knowledge you share.

Ancestors, we honor you!

Honoring the Nature Spirits

Nature Spirits, you live all around us. Thank you for being part of our ecosystem.
Nature Spirits, we honor you!

Honoring the Shining Ones

Shining Ones, you are bright and powerful. Thank you for guiding us.
Shining Ones, we honor you!

Honoring the Being of the Occasion

[Spirit], we welcome you today to celebrate [holiday]. This is the time of year when…. [seasonal description]

[Spirit], we honor you!

Prayer of Sacrifice

We've honored a lot of spirits today, and would like to make one last offering to them.
Spirits all, we honor you!

Taking the Omen

We've made offerings to [Spirit]. Let's see what they have to say to us:

*this can be done in many ways. You may choose to pull a card and have the child explain what they see in the picture. You may use a symbol set and explain the meaning of the pulled symbol to the child. You may choose to listen to nature and see what you hear/see/feel.

Return Flow

Now it's time to share our [food/drink]. The spirits joined us here today, and we're going to celebrate the blessings they share with us. Let's put those blessings into this [food/drink]. Rub your hands together until they feel warm. Now hold your [food/drink] and feel that heat go into it. With our energy, and the spirits help, our [food/drink] is now blessed. Let's [eat/drink] it!

Thanking the Spirits

Ancestors, Nature Spirits, Shining Ones, [Being of the Occasion], We had a great time at this ritual with you. Thanks for joining us for this special day.
Spirits all, we thank you!

Closing the Gates

We now call out to our Gatekeeper to help us close the gates since we're done with our ritual. Gatekeeper, [or specific spirit], be here with us. Let our Fire close as a gate. Let our Well close as a gate. Let our Tree close as a gate.

Let the Gates be Closed!

Thanking the Earth Mother

Earth Mother, we know you're always around us. Thanks for joining us for this special day.
Earth Mother, we thank you!

Recessional

Now our ritual is over. It's time to clean up and leave our ritual space.

Optional: sing "Go With the Fire" by Mike Bierschenk
Go with the light of the fire inside you.

Go with the might of the Gods to guide you.
Go with the Ancestors beside you.
Go with the Fire.

Resources & Further Reading

There are a fair number of resources out there for raising your child in a pagan tradition, getting them connected to nature, and introducing them to mythology. Many of these resources are covered in the Reading Extensions each week, but there are other more general resources that are helpful, and often hard to find. Some of these are geared towards kids, and some are geared towards parents. Many of the books and resources here are written from a Wiccan perspective, so if you follow another pagan tradition, you'll have to adapt them to your needs.

General Resources

Little Pagan Acorns at http://www.littlepaganacorns.com
- A collection of printable worksheets and activities. Leans Wiccan

Rupert's Tales series by Kyrja
- There is a book for each of the 8 High Days. Leans Wiccan

Charter Oak Grove, ADF's Family Resources at https://charteroakadf.org/family-resources/
- A collection of leveled readers and ritual scripts for each of the 8 High Days. Leans Druidic

The Family Virtues Guide: Simple Ways to Bring Out the Best in Our Children and Ourselves by Linda Kavelin Popov
- Interfaith book with 52 virtues. Is monotheistic in its approach, but adaptable to a polytheistic worldview

Books on Pagan Parenting

Circle Round: Raising Children in Goddess Traditions by Starhawk, Diane Baker, & Anne Hill
- A well-rounded book structured around the 8 High Days, containing activities, rituals, songs, and recipes.

Also contains information on rites of passage and the 4 elements. Leans Wiccan

Pagan Parenting: Spiritual, Magical, and Emotional Development of the Child by Kristin Madden
- Includes exercises, games, and rituals, as well as advice on how to approach raising a pagan child in a majority monotheistic world.

Parenting Pagan Tots by Janet Callahan
- Geared towards new parents. Collection of activities for building pagan family traditions. Suggestions on how to handle mainstream holidays.

Mythology

Treasury of Greek Mythology by Donna Jo Napoli

Treasury of Norse Mythology by Donna Jo Napoli

Celtic Mythology by Philip Freeman

Myths, Legends, & Sacred Stories by Philip Wilkinson

Celtic Mythology: History for Kids by Dinobibi Publishing

Z is for Zeus: A Greek Mythology Alphabet by Helen L Wilbur

D'Aulaires' Book of Norse Myths by Ingri and Edgar Parin d'Aulaire

D'Aulaires' Book of Greek Myths by Ingri and Edgar Parin d'Aulaire

Usborne Greek Myths for Young Children by Heather Amery

Tales from the Mabinogion by Gwyn Thomas

Heroes, Gods, and Emperors from Roman Mythology by Kerry Usher

Connecting to Nature

The Last Child in the Woods by Richard Louv
- Talks about how children today are kept inside more, the dangers of that, as well as suggestions for helping kids and parents get back out into nature

A Little Bit of Dirt: 55+ Science & Art Activities to Reconnect Children with Nature by Asia Citro
- Collection of experiments and outdoor activities. Any materials used are common household items, or easy to get from a grocery store.

[State] Nature Set: Field Guides to Wildlife, Birds, Trees & Wildflowers of [State] by James Kavanagh
- There is one for each of the US States, and some Canadian provinces. Three laminated pamphlets that are a great introduction to field guides, and easy & light to take on walks.